AF375230

Josiah and Naiyah's World

Sensory Processing Disorder

Katrina J. Howard &
Josiah Howard-Tobia

DEDICATION

This book is dedicated to all the people who help us live a life with fewer meltdowns. Thank you to our teachers ,therapists, and our infant developmental specialist. Thank you for caring about the quality of life for children/families like us. Thank you for teaching coping strategies and how to regulate our emotions. Thank you for teaching communication (verbal and nonverbal) and daily living skills. Thank you for being you!

Thank you to our family and friends who help Mommy when she needs it. Thank you for watching us so Mommy can recharge her battery and be the best mommy she can be. Thank you for going on day trips or vacations with us so Mommy has the extra hands in case we are a handful. We love and appreciate you all.

Hi, Guys! Josiah and Naiyah here. Today we want to tell you a little about sensory processing disorder, or **SPD** for short. Just like autism, sensory processing disorder can show itself in many ways. My sister and I both have **SPD**. I also have autism. I told you a little about my autism in *Josiah's Ausome Adventures: My Autism*. I hope you got a chance to read it.

One way that sensory processing disorder can show up and cause a challenge for children is loud noises. Naiyah and I don't like the sound of fireworks, dogs barking, the vacuum cleaner, sirens, or loud music. Those are just some things. Being outside where there are a lot of noises all at once can cause us to have something called sensory overload meltdown. The funny thing is we can be the loudest people in a room and often don't realize it.

Sometimes we have to wear our ear defenders to keep us calm. Ear defenders look like the things airport or construction workers wear to protect their ears. I don't like when people stare and point. It's rude and makes us feel like something is wrong with us or different about us. We're just like everyone else, except our senses can get overloaded.

For some kids with sensory processing disorder, staring and making comments makes the meltdown worse and last longer. It's best to be kind and ask as if nothing is happening. People don't stare and laugh at construction workers when they wear their ear protection. Why do people do that to us when we wear ours? Mommy prefers that people ask questions if they are curious. Usually there are no dumb questions. If you don't know, you don't know.

Another way sensory processing disorder can show up for kids with SPD is not liking the texture or smell of foods. Being offered something to eat that feels or smells weird can cause sensory overstimulation. When it comes to our food, we may be extremely picky eaters or grazers. Grazing means we don't eat a lot at once but are constantly snacking. In severe cases we may not eat at all. It's not as easy as thinking, "We'll eat when we get hungry enough." Kids with SPD may have an allergy to the food or something going on inside their throats or tummies that makes them reject the food.

To me, some foods have weird textures, funny smells, and strong flavors, so I won't eat them. It is very hard for me to eat vegetables and some meats but I love fruits and sweets. That makes it hard for my mommy to find things for me to eat. She gets worried about my diet and my weight. I am getting better with that! I now try new foods at least a few times. Mommy says I have to try at least one "no thank you" bite with each new item on my plate. It's okay not to like it, but I have to try it.

Naiyah is the same way when it comes to food. She has a very limited diet. She only likes fruit, sweets, dairy, and bread. She might eat other things, but not much. She also likes to play with her food but doesn't like the feel of it on her hands. Seems strange, right? Playing with the food feeds her sensory needs, but having dirty hands doesn't. That part bothers her and makes her have a meltdown.

Sometimes Naiyah throws her food or plate when she's frustrated. You can imagine a bowl of oatmeal on the floor is a mess to clean! Naiyah also shoves food in her mouth and has started to chew on ice. These behaviors are common for children with sensory processing disorder.

When it comes to sensory processing disorder and clothes, I don't like certain fabrics or tags. My mommy has to cut those tags out. If she doesn't, I feel itchy and scratchy and can't focus on anything else. I have gotten better with my clothes, but I still prefer certain fabrics, shorts, and short-sleeve shirts. It doesn't matter what season it is. That's how I'm most comfortable. In the middle of winter I put on shorts and T-shirts before long sleeves and pants. Good thing we don't have freezing winters here! I'm not sure that would even matter.

For Naiyah, sensory processing disorder causes her to feel uncomfortable in clothes. The clothes bother her so much that she doesn't like to wear any! She's always taking her clothes off and running around the house. Sometimes she even takes off her diaper. Mommy has to chase Naiyah to put them back on. That's funny to me but can be very serious. It's very common for kids with SPD to not like wearing clothes, go barefoot, and sometimes take their clothes off at inappropriate times. So far, Naiyah keeps her clothes on in public.

For my sister and me, having sensory processing disorder means sometimes we like to chew on inedible things like our clothes, paper, or toys. Mommy bought us something called "chewies" so we get the texture, oral stimulation, and sensations without chewing on harmful things. I have chewed holes in many shirts in the past. I don't know why we like to chew so much, but it feels good. We also like to suck our thumbs to soothe ourselves when we are overloaded or tired.

Sensory processing disorder can make simple daily tasks like diaper changes, hair brushing, toothbrushing, hair washing, and haircuts hard for children. Since birth I have had a hard time with hair washing, brushing, and getting haircuts. I used to have a really hard time with toothbrushing, but I have gotten so much better as I've gotten older. Mommy cuts my hair, and now that I like getting my whole head wet, I like getting my hair washed. I'm so proud of myself. Little steps are steps!

Naiyah has a really hard time dealing with all of those things, to the point of severe meltdowns. She hits, screams, and cries until Mommy stops and gives her a chance to calm down. Mommy then has to do a massage or something soothing to be able to finish the tasks. I hope Naiyah gets better with those things as she gets older. Therapists and specialists help Sister with her daily living skills. I try to help her too!

Feeding our sensory diet helps a lot with all of those tasks. A sensory diet is a set of activities that provide sensory input to help us stay focused or calm down. The activities are individual to the person. One way Naiyah and I feed our sensory diet is to play with squishy things like slime, kinetic sand, and cloud dough. We love to jump on a trampoline, flip on a bar, or tumble on a gym mat. We also play in water, chase bubbles, and spin.

My sensory diet activities are not always the same as Naiyah's. Sometimes we enjoy the same things, and other times she may need something more. She does something called heavy work when she needs to calm down. That's just what it sounds like. She will move heavy objects by pushing them around the room or stacking and unstacking them. It calms and centers her body to help regulate her moods and behavior.

Sometimes when I'm out in public I may spin, jump, and flap my arms. Those are called stims. Stims are repetitive or unusual body movements or noises that help calm me down. When I'm stimming and people stare, that makes me and my mommy feel funny. Just like when I'm wearing my ear defenders, we would rather people ask, and I can tell them I have autism and sensory processing disorder.

When Naiyah is in public and she has really bad meltdowns, people think she's misbehaving or having a tantrum. A sensory meltdown is not the same as a tantrum. You cannot discipline a sensory meltdown. When Naiyah has a meltdown, it means she is in overload, and she needs a break to calm down and regulate her behavior. Giving unsolicited advice to a parent or caregiver does not help the situation. If you see this happening, it's best to ignore the meltdown or offer help to keep the child safe and give the parent a break.

One of the things I like to do is get "arm or feet time" with Mommy. I like to rub her arm or leg while sucking my thumb. Mommy has said that I can only do this at home unless it is absolutely necessary to calm down in public. I like to rub Mommy's arm when we are doing things like flying or riding a shuttle because I hate traveling. When Mommy lets me have "arm time" it relaxes me and helps me feel safe.

Sleep issues are another common challenge for children with SPD. When I was a baby and toddler, I had a hard time falling and staying asleep. I'd cry myself to sleep and wake constantly through the night. It wasn't the normal baby waking. I just couldn't get my body settled to fall asleep. Naiyah was the same and worse. She wouldn't just cry but would scream and stay awake through the night. She's finally starting to rest even if she doesn't sleep. No sleep makes a cranky little one the next morning.

One of the biggest challenges for kids with SPD is trouble with transitions. We can have a hard time stopping one activity and moving on to another. We require time to switch activities. Otherwise we might have a meltdown. We aren't trying to be naughty. It just takes our brains a little longer to prepare for something new. That's also one of the reasons we have trouble with sharing.

Those are some struggles with sensory processing disorder. If you see a child like me or my sister, please be kind. It's always nice to be nice. If any family members, friends, or classmates have SPD please help them by not making them feel weird or different because of the stimming they do. Sensory processing disorder creates behaviors we cannot control.

I hope we helped you learn about sensory process-ing disorder. Thanks for coming into Naiyah's and my world for a little bit. Please share what you learned with your friends and family to make the world more inclusive for children like us. We are much like you. The only difference is we need a little more help to navigate our surroundings. Bye for now!